The
Affirmations
Coloring
Book

The Affirmations Coloring Book

Compiled by
Felicity James

SIRIUS

SIRIUS

This edition published in 2019 by Sirius Publishing, a division of
Arcturus Publishing Limited,
26/27 Bickels Yard, 151–153 Bermondsey Street,
London SE1 3HA

ISBN: 978-1-78888-767-0
AD006756NT

Printed in China

Introduction

Coloring in is the perfect way to relax, create, and bring about a calmer, happier state of mind. This book contains gorgeous images to color and make your own, alongside affirmative phrases and quotes designed to inspire and uplift you.

Breathe life into these floral and geometric patterns by completing them in colors of your choosing. Some of the affirmations can themselves be colored in, allowing you to focus more deeply on the positive message. Use pens, felt-tips, markers or pencils for bright, vivid hues or a subtler style of shading—whatever feels right for you.

I have the power
to change my life.

*I have the courage
to follow my dreams.*

I'm passionately involved in life:
I love its change,
its colour, its movement.

Arthur Rubinstein

I am worthy of love
and happiness.

The future belongs to those who believe in the beauty of their dreams.

Eleanor Roosevelt

I focus on the moment and let everything else wash away.

I am loved by family
and friends.

Follow your inner moonlight;
don't hide the madness.

Allen Ginsberg

*I was born to make mistakes,
not to fake perfection.*

Drake

I choose forgiveness
over anger.

I love feeling alive,
I love walking out in the cold
in my bare feet and
feeling the ice on my toes.

Tori Amos

I have all the wealth I need.

I can be changed by what happens to me.
But I refuse to be reduced by it.

Maya Angelou

Each day I am rejuvenated

I know where I'm going and
I know the truth, and I don't have
to be what you want me to be.
I'm free to be what I want.

Muhammad Ali

Make the self your refuge
and your lamp.

Buddha

*I embrace optimism
and a positive attitude.*

I love myself for who I am,
not for who I could be.

I believe in living today.
Not in yesterday,
nor in tomorrow.

Loretta Young

I have tremendous faith
in the universe. I feel at home on this
planet. Even though it's
a very big world out there,
I plan on walking right through
the middle of it, unharmed.

Marion Ross

I always strive to be
the best version of myself.

It always seems impossible
until it's done.

Nelson Mandela

The best preparation for tomorrow is doing your best for today.

H. Jackson Brown Jr

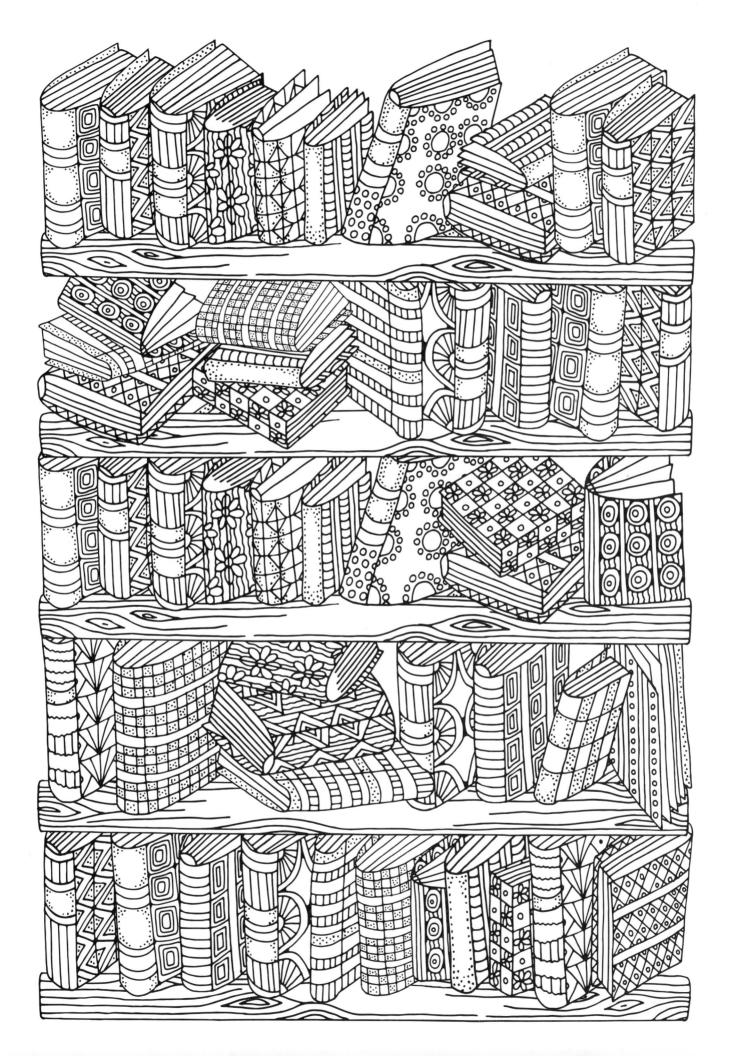

I admire others' beauty without questioning my own.

Live your beliefs and
you can turn the world around.

Henry David Thoreau

Whatever makes you uncomfortable is your biggest opportunity for growth.
Bryant McGill

The most authentic thing about us
is our capacity to create,
to overcome, to endure,
to transform, to love and
to be greater than our suffering.

Ben Okri

In a gentle way,
you can shake the world.

Mahatma Gandhi

*If you haven't found it yet,
keep looking.*

Steve Jobs

I give my best in all I do

Believe that life is worth living
and your belief will help
create the fact.

William James

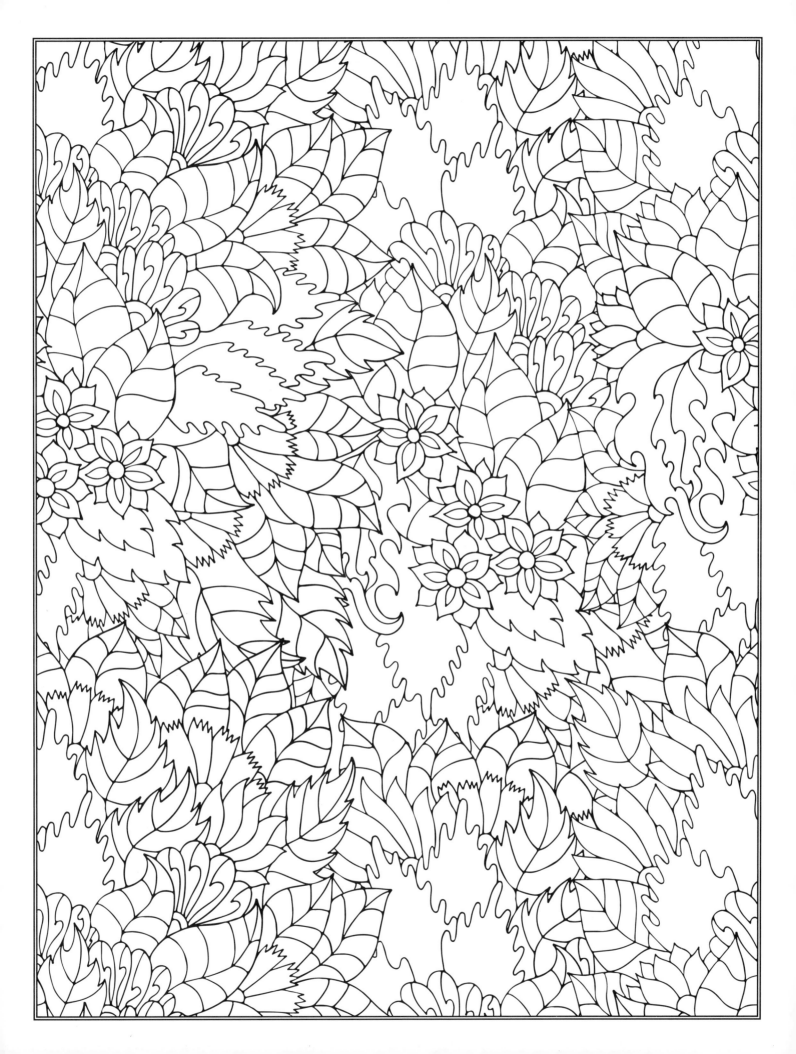

I delight in the simple things in life.

I am ready for any situation
and stand firm in the storm.

I believe in the impossible because no one else does.

Florence Griffith Joyner

Respect yourself and others
will respect you.

Confucius

My flaws make me unique

Love yourself.
It is important to stay positive because
beauty comes from the inside out.

Jenn Proske

I believe in and trust
my own judgement.

I take responsibility for my actions, both good and bad.

The only journey is the one within.

Rainer Maria Rilke

I am in control of my feelings
and actions.

I am deliberate and afraid of nothing.

Audre Lorde

Choose, everyday, to forgive yourself.
You are human, flawed and, most of
all, worthy of love.

Alison Malee

I do
not dwell
on the
faults of
others

I am resilient in the face
of challenges.

Do not mind anything that anyone tells you about anyone else. Judge everyone and everything for yourself.

Henry James

I readily accept and appreciate constructive criticism.

I let go of what I am,
I become what I might be.

Lao Tzu

I make time to meditate on peace.

Most of us have far more courage than we ever dreamed we possessed.

Dale Carnegie

*I listen to my heart
and follow my intuition.*

You are braver than you believe,
stronger than you seem,
and smarter than you think.

A. A. Milne

I keep busy with my own affairs
and not those of others.

Looking behind, I am filled
with gratitude. Looking forward,
I am filled with vision. Looking upwards,
I am filled with strength.
Looking within, I discover peace.

Apache prayer

My life is a gift.
I will use this gift with confidence,
joy and exuberance.

I want to make this world perfect.

Malala Yousafzai

May I be I is the only prayer.

E. E. Cummings

I accept small irritations
with good humour.

I hope that I may always desire more than I can accomplish.

Michelangelo

My mind is clear
and my heart is strong.

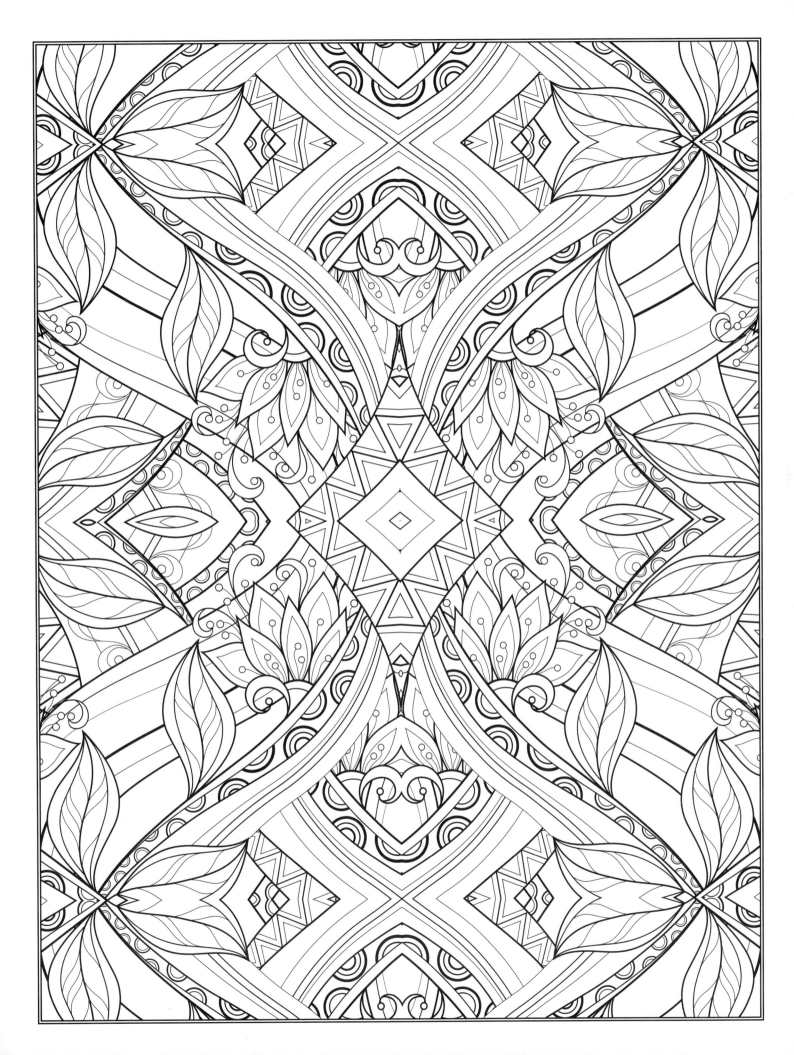

Be true to yourself and surround yourself with positive, supportive people.

Payal Kadakia

There is only one happiness in this life,
to love and be loved.

George Sand

Turn your face to the sun
and the shadow falls behind you.

Jan Goldstein

I am compassionate and thoughtful.

At the end of the day,
love and compassion will win.

Terry Waite